The Farmer's Son

Further titles in this series

A Busker on Bow Street

Lost Dreams

The Seasonal Visitor

The Farmer's Son

Short Stories for Adult Learners No. 3

LinguaBooks Readers

Copyright © 2018 LinguaBooks

The right of the individual authors to be identified as the authors of the stories included in this collection has been asserted in accordance with sections 77 and 78 of the Copyright, Designs and Patents Act 1988.

Published in the United Kingdom by LinguaBooks

ISBN: 978-1-911369-12-7

A CIP catalogue record for this book is available from the British Library.

Series editor: Maurice Claypole
Edited by: Ann Claypole
Proofreader: Marie-Christin Strobel

LinguaBooks
Elsie Whiteley Innovation Centre
Hopwood Lane, Halifax HX1 5ER
www.linguabooks.com

The universe is made of stories, not atoms.

– Muriel Rukeyser

ACKNOWLEDGEMENTS

Some of these stories first appeared in *The Written Word*, a journal for English-speaking residents of Baden-Württemberg, Germany.

The publishers would like to thank the authors of the original stories for offering their work for publication and similarly to express their gratitude to all who were involved in producing both *The Written Word* and the present collection, thereby enabling these stories to reach a wider audience within the context of adult literacy and language learning.

Image credits: cover, page 8, 19, 31, 41, 53 Dreamstime; 18, 30, 52, 64 pixabay; 42 Mr Punch's Book of Sports; 46 ClipartXtras

Contents

Introduction

This LinguaBooks Reader is the third volume of short stories to be published in this innovative new series.

The stories are presented as originally written by native speakers of English from a variety of countries and backgrounds. Although the punctuation and spelling have largely been harmonised, no attempt has been made to simplify or sanitise the language used. The main objective here is to give learners and other readers an authentic language experience whilst at the same time providing plenty of scope for language acquisition, enhanced awareness and vocabulary expansion. From a point of view of difficulty, the language varies in terms of complexity and register and may be considered equivalent to Level C1 of the Common European Framework of Reference for Languages (CEFR).

The content and scope make each book in this series ideal for classroom use, but the stories can also be read for pleasure, with or without recourse to the supplementary material included. The words and phrases explained after each story provide useful assistance, but lay no claim to completeness, since learners nowadays have ready access to a wide range of external resources. Autonomous learners who favour an active approach will also benefit from the activities and puzzles, which represent a combination of consolidation and discovery exercises. An answer key is provided for the convenience of learners, teachers and independent readers.

The Farmer's Son

by Anthony Curtis

— ❧ ❧ —

I met him at a farm. He didn't need to chew a straw; his bleary, bulging eyes that never seemed to be able to focus on any particular point, his idiot grin and his red, weather-beaten face, which he never seemed to have washed, told their own story.

And everybody loved him.

His secret, if he ever had one, was that he loved everybody and everything. He couldn't think bad thinks (his own words).

One day he told me that he had only one enemy in the world, and that was himself. I was the second, but he never knew it.

The girls laughed at him and he drooled at the girls, and I believe that if an atom bomb had exploded under his feet, he would have emerged from the catastrophe grinning broadly, saying that the world was just having its little joke.

His parents adored him. They told me that he had never been sick in his life, that he walked in the footsteps of saints, and that he would live for ever.

He worked on his parents' farm, which was ninety percent horses and ten percent chickens. His job was to feed the horses, so he was occupied for most of the day.

I had no choice but to lodge at the farm, for it was the only cheap accommodation available in those parts. My boss at the office was too stingy to allow me an expense account, so every evening I ate with the family at the farm. This meant sitting opposite him as he shovelled home-cooked food into his foolish face.

More than once, I asked myself, "He's just a country bumpkin. Why should I bother with him at all?"

I knew the answer, of course. He was better than I was. Thinking of all the petty crimes I had committed in my life, I knew I was not worthy to step into his muddy boots.

"What is it that makes you so ugly?" I asked him once – rather cruelly, I must admit.

"Ugliness is in the eye of the beholder," was his answer, and I turned my back on him and quickly walked away, for I realised with a shock that I had met my match – in a country bumpkin.

In retrospect, I think it's quite likely that I would eventually have done him in, for I hated his smugness, but as it happened, someone, or rather something, did the job for me.

One evening I came back from the office and he wasn't there.

"'E's in the 'ospital," said the father.

"A 'orse bit 'e," said the mother.

"Why aren't you with him, then?" I asked.

"Don't you worry none, 'e ain't gonna die," said the father.

I found out the name of the hospital and drove there without a moment's hesitation, breaking the speed limit all the way.

The horse had bitten him in the neck.

"You said you never think bad thinks," I said. "What about the horse? He bit you didn't he? You must be thinking bad thinks about him."

"No," said the bumpkin, and I had to lean over to catch his words.

 "You've got it orl wrong. If the horse 'ad 'ated me, he would've kicked me to death. It was a love bite. 'E didn't know 'is own strength…"

And with those words he ascended into heaven.

My boss at the office has a new assistant now.

The old couple feed the ten percent chickens. I feed the ninety percent horses. In the evenings, I sit at the supper table and eat in silence, while the mother and father finger their rosaries and pray for the return of their son.

— ❧ ❧ —

Words and phrases

bleary	watery, unable to see clearly
bulging	sticking out, protruding
thinks	primitive word for thoughts
drooled	dribbled saliva as a sign of desire
occupied	busy doing things
lodge	rent a room
accommodation	somewhere to live or stay
stingy	mean, unwilling to spend money
country bumpkin	awkward or simple person from the countryside
bother	concern myself
petty	lesser, trivial
not worthy to step in his muddy boots	not as good a person as he was
in the eye of the beholder	a matter of personal opinion
met my match	was competing with someone as good as or better than me
in retrospect	thinking back
done him in	murdered him
smugness	self-satisfaction, excessive pride
catch his words	hear him
rosaries	strings of beads used for counting prayers

Food for thought

1. Why does the narrator say, *'He didn't need to chew a straw.'*?
   a. Because chewing a straw is thought to be an action typical of simple country folk.
   b. To illustrate that farmer's son was never hungry.
   c. As an indication of affection.

2. *'He couldn't think bad thinks.'* What is special about this sentence?
   a. It shows that the farmer's son does not always tell the truth.
   b. The writer is trying to use poetic language.
   c. The word 'thinks' is not normally used in this way.

3. Speaking of the farmer's son, which of the following statements is true?
   a. His parents thought he was a saint.
   b. His father and mother loved him.
   c. His parents made him work too hard.

4. *'Ugliness is in the eye of the beholder.'* This is a variation on a more common expression. Which of the following would you normally expect to hear?
   a. Ugliness is in the eye of the onlooker.
   b. Ugliness is in the sight of the beholder.
   c. Beauty is in the eye of the beholder.

5. At the end of the story, the narrator has taken the place of the farmer's son. Why did he do this?
   a. He is hiding from the police.
   b. The events on the farm have changed his attitude to life in some way.
   c. He believes the farmer's son will come back.

Crossword puzzle

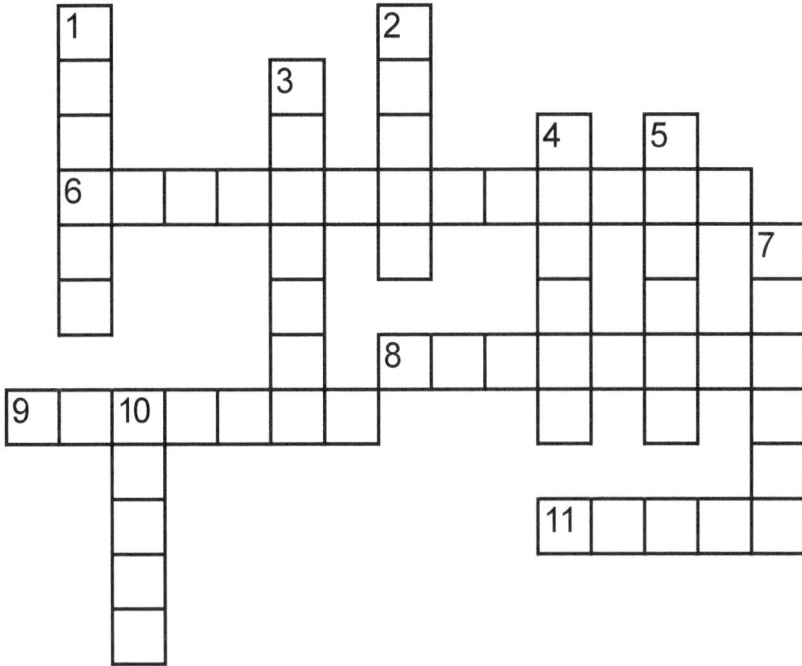

ACROSS

6 somewhere to live
8 self-satisfaction
9 sticking out
11 trivial

DOWN

1 watery (eyes)
2 dribble, saliva
3 country person
4 mean
5 concern oneself
7 string of beads
10 rent a room

Picture quiz – farm animals

A Name the animals shown below (they are not mentioned in the story). Use the initial letters given.

1

2

3

4

5

6

1 D_____   **2** T_____   **3** P _____

4 R_____   **5** C_____   **6** D_____

B Match the sounds with the animals-
1 oink ( ) **2** hee-haw ( ) **3** quack ( )
4 moo ( ) **5** cock-a-doodle-doo ( ) **6** gobble ( )

The Scarlet Dress

by Arja Faller-Nenonen

— ❧ ❧ —

My mother ran a small but exclusive dressmaking business. I could sit in the waiting room doing my homework or flicking through the latest Paris fashion magazines for hours, observing the comings and goings of the customers at the same time. My favourite fashions were the bridal and evening dresses, which I studied and copied for the princesses I liked to draw. They were far more glamorous and beautiful than any of my mother's customers, who were often wealthy, but disappointingly for me, neither young and glamorous nor beautiful.

When my mother told me that there was a dress to be delivered, I was always very keen to go anywhere. I was a curious child. I loved being sent to posh houses to deliver dresses. Most customers liked to collect theirs in person in order to try them on before they paid and took them away. But there were a few even more exclusive clients who totally trusted my mother and wanted their dresses delivered. One of these was a small round lady, the wife of a famous portrait artist called Alfred Alopeus. She always presented my mother with the most amazing new fabrics, which was very unusual in 1949, when most mortals were lucky to have any fabric at all for a new dress. Very often a customer would bring two old dresses which were carefully picked apart and, under my mother's clever design skills, transformed into one fashionable dress. Mrs

Alopeus' fabrics were different – exotic fabrics in brilliant colours. For me, it was like watching a magician pull a white rabbit out of a hat when Mrs Alopeus came and opened her bag and pulled out another fantastic silk, causing a lot of oohs and aahs from the 'girls'. Mother told us that the lady's nephew was the Finnish ambassador to Peking, which was supposed to explain it all.

This time the fabric was of brilliant red satin. The dress was deeply décolleté with enormous puff sleeves and a very wide long skirt, which had eaten up miles of fabric. It was carefully packed in a cardboard box with tissue paper between the folds. The Alopeuses lived in a part of town which had been spared the air raids. It was called Eira, which reminded me of the opera. My mother was an opera fan and I knew of a famous Finnish singer, Maria Eira, who seldom appeared in her native country. Eira is still one of the poshest parts of Helsinki, crammed with houses built in the Finnish National Romantic style. They were made of huge grey or red granite blocks and carved with fantastic ornaments. I loved having an excuse to go there. It was a long tram journey and I held the box with the scarlet satin dress in my arms as if it were a baby. My arms ached. This was an important mission for me and I had to come home with money in my pocket.

There before me was a huge grey-granite edifice with a turret. I checked and double checked the address. The place looked like a palace. I would have liked to be a princess shut up in there. I was twelve and a hopeless romantic, drawing castles on steep mountains with princes and princesses. Now I was about to enter one of my dream castles.

I watched the house for an eternity before I rang the bell. A maid opened the door.

"I have a dress to deliver," I whispered conspiratorially.

"Oh yes, I know. Just wait a moment," the maid said and left me standing in a huge entrance hall with parquet floor and Persian carpets.

An enormous chandelier hung from the ceiling and up on one wall was a full-length portrait of a beautiful young lady wearing the same dress that I was delivering.

I said to myself, "It really is the same dress, the same fabric, the same style, the same model."

But the lady in the portrait was young and slim and beautiful. She looked like a younger version of Mrs Alopeus. Could it be her daughter? Just at that moment, an elderly man appeared. He had a goatee beard, long grey hair and spectacles. He wore grey tweeds, such as I always imagined Englishmen to wear when hunting.

He said, with a slight foreign accent, "I see you admire the portrait of my wife. She is very beautiful. I do not need any other models."

This puzzled me more. Either my eyes were playing tricks on me, or I was dreaming. The old man did not even look at the dress and I did not see Mrs Alopeus at all. I handed him the dress box and presented the bill. I was paid and given a handsome tip.

Before I could open my mouth to form a question, I was out in the street again. I didn't take the tram but walked all the way home thinking about the portrait and the dress. Mother wondered where on earth I had been. She had been worried about me, but was glad I was home safe with the money. When I told her about the portrait, she laughed and said I had imagined it all, and that I had read too many fairy tales.

We never saw Mrs Alopeus again, nor heard anything of her artist husband, but the image of that portrait remains forever imprinted on my memory.

— ❧ ❧ —

Words and phrases

exclusive	not available to everyone
dressmaking	making clothes for women and girls
glamorous	more attractive or interesting than ordinary people
posh	elegant, fashionable
portrait	painting or drawing of a person
fabrics	cloth or materials
most mortals	ordinary people
picked apart	separated into pieces
fashionable	popular at the time
'girls'	women working at the dressmakers'
eaten up miles of fabric	used a lot of material
crammed with	packed with
huge	extremely large
granite	hard rock used in building
edifice	building
turret	small narrow tower
maid	female servant
tweeds	clothes of thick woollen cloth
imagined	pictured in my mind
a handsome tip	a generous extra payment

Food for thought

1. Which is the best description of the girl in the story?
   a. She wanted to become a dressmaker.
   b. She loved romantic stories and settings.
   c. She was a dreamer who never did any school work.

2. Why did most customers like to collect their dresses in person?
   a. The girl's mother wanted them to try the dresses on before they took them away.
   b. They liked to spend a lot of time at the dressmaker's.
   c. They didn't want to risk paying for something that was not quite right.

3. Why did some customers bring old dresses?
   a. Times were hard and material was scarce.
   b. Fashions changed so fast that they could no longer wear the old dresses.
   c. They wanted to watch the dressmaker take them apart.

4. Where did the Alopeuses live?
   a. in an ambassador's residence
   b. in a very fashionable part of Helsinki
   c. in a palatial castle with turrets

5. Who is the lady in the portrait?
   a. Mrs Alopeus
   b. Mrs Alopeus' daughter
   c. We never find out.

Word search

Find the words in the grid. Words can go horizontally, vertically or diagonally in any direction.

```
X  M     Q  H  N  D     P  C  R  A  M  M  E  D     Y
T  M  L  T  Q  P  P  E  B  W  M  D  H     N  Y  W  V
X  V  D  C  E  O  T  V     E  M  O  S  D  N  A  H  Y
K  R  F  F  M  R  T  I  T  N  X  V  V  I  V  D     Y
D  X  G  F  K  T  R  S  X  D  C  J  L  A  K  G  N  J
H  M  R  T  C  R  P  U  B  R  B  F  H  M  N     E  K
Z  U  K  M  K  A  Y  L  T  V  C  C  F  I  S  D     Z
P  X  G  N  T  I  J  C  R  D  L  A  K  D  I  G  T  B
M  T  D  E  N  T  F  X  V  J  B  A  E  F  R  R  R
R  K  L  K        N  E     R  M  E  I  N  L  A  A  D
V  F  T  W  P  N  N  C  I  S  W  C  H  M  Z  N  P  E
W  Q  Q  N  Y  O  I  C  S  T  E  W  R  F  R  I  A  N
G  B  M  R  P  R  S  E  Z     V  F  F  T  N  T  D  I
N  D  M  R  B     R  H  G  F  V  V  X  T  C  E  E  G
H  X  G  A  T  D  M  Z        N  K  V  W  P     K  A
G  G  F  M  G  L  A  M  O  R  O  U  S     K  H  C  M
K     S  L  A  T  R  O  M  T  S  O  M  K  N  C  I  I
G     E  L  B  A  N  O  I  H  S  A  F  M  N  Z  P  D
```

crammed	fashionable	imagined	apart
dressmaking	glamorous	maid	portrait
edifice	granite	most	posh
exclusive	handsome	mortals	turret
fabric	huge	picked	tweeds

Picture quiz – ladies' clothing

A Name the items of clothing shown below. Use the initial letters given.

1   2   3

4   5   6

1 S_____ **2** B_____ **3** B_____

4 D_____ **5** C_____ **6** T_____

B Which of the above…
1 is worn full-length ( ) **2** hangs from the waist ( )
3 has lapels ( ) **4** is slipped over the head ( )
5 pulls in the waist ( ) **6** has shoulder straps ( )

Ghostly Laughter

by Shelly Bowers

—— ❧ ❧ ——

Come and sit yourself down here. You're after stories of fairies, are ye? Now, why would you be after stories of fairies, then? Ah! A thesis no less. One of those college types, are ye?

Ye've come to the right God-forsaken hole to hear of fairies. Every man and woman in this pub has a tale to tell of those beautiful dangerous people and what's more, they'll be fallin' over each other to tell it to ye. But you take it easy; it's a flippant type that talks easily of the fairy folk.

Have I met them, eh? Well, that's a question, Would you believe me if I had? Oh, so you don't believe. Well, why should I tell you if you don't believe? Better than that, why would you want to know if you don't believe? A sociological study, you say. But what would I know of that? Then again, what would I know of what I saw. Let's say I don't know if I've ever seen fairies, but I've seen something that I don't think many have seen.

Well, I know if you want to hear of that I think that I'd better wet my throat. Mine's a Guinness and a Paddy's; I know a lot of lasses are on the Bailey's now, but that sweet stuff ain't for me. Talking's thirsty work, if you know what I mean.

May God bless you for the drink. Now, let's go and sit by the fire. That's it, make yourself comfy by the last blessed turf fire in Ireland and I'll tell of my fairy folk.

I was born in 1950, yes it seems a lifetime ago. My parents had lived through the war and scenes of the Belfast Blitz were seared into their memories. They had seen hundreds blown to kingdom come and for that very reason every Sunday during the fine summer weather we became pilgrims to the war memorial to remember the men who gave life and freedom to Ireland, Britain, Europe and the world with their souls, their bodies and their youth.

Anyway, Sunday when I was a child was Memorial Day. We gave thanks for our lives and our families, but I was there for the sun, the grass and the roses, twirling with my hands in the air and as my dress lifted, I would find myself rising into the sky above the great oaks.

In circles I would spin, higher and higher until I could reach the clouds and touch their cotton wool with my fingertips. Then fall to the earth and lie on the green, with rose petals for a pillow and the sky revolving over my head. It was then that they would come to play, those beautiful girls. They were older, but they called me by my name. Mary, come and play. Mary, come and dance. I raised my head from the grass and saw they were beautiful and wore dresses of fresh poppies. They had lips rouged with blood, porcelain white skin and long dark tresses as black as funeral ribbon.

They danced, skipped and laughed, giggled, laughed and sang, laughed and danced. They would take me by my tiny hands and we would play ring-a-ring-a-roses, as their dark long curls flew in the breeze and the sun grew warm in the sky. Their faces, those of loved ones, cousins, sisters, daughters never known, but near, unborn but alive. My tiny hands in the sisters', I would dance and remember the pain and fear, the hurt and the death of war, but more than that, we danced and laughed for life: the life of the lost men.

We would dance round the obelisk and chant the names of the soldiers and with each name, the life of love, laughter and happiness would flow. This was the lost feelings of a lifetime cut short, a lost ghost.

I would dance in fear, but the sisters would smooth my dark curly hair and laugh, lift me high in the air and sing soothingly of lost love and children unknown to me. They would weave daisies in my hair and hang garlands of poppies around my soft white neck, hug and love me as a lost child, throw rose petals at my feet and spread their arms wide for my hugs when my chubby little arms spread forth for acceptance, to embrace the love unfulfilled.

Then the shadow would come, the sun would die and my Granda would come to lift me into his huge shipbuilder's arms and say "Enough". The sisters cringed in his sight, clinging to the obelisk as he raised his staff of hawthorn. All would flee before his wrath.

My sisters would fly leaving only the sad wreaths of death, paper poppies crumbling dry in the wind, leaving me alone in the evening light – alone under the shadow of the obelisk, without the love, without the song, without the dance, with only the echo of ghostly laughter.

I am the child the fairies didn't steal.

— ❦ ❧ —

Words and phrases

thesis	written research report
God-forsaken hole	boring, depressing place
flippant	not serious enough
turf	peat, vegetable matter used as fuel
blown to kingdom come	killed in an explosion
pilgrims	people who go to a holy place
war memorial	monument to those who died in war
twirling	turning around and around
spin	turn around a central point
revolving	moving around a central axis
rouged	coloured red
porcelain white	pure white
tresses	long flowing hair
obelisk	tall pillar or shaft of stone
chant	repeat over and over again
garlands	decoration made of flowers and/or leaves
embrace	accept
cringed	drew back in fear
staff	wooden stick
wreath	circular decoration made of flowers and/or leaves, traditionally laid at war memorials

Food for thought

1. Who is the speaker addressing in this story?
   a. an investigative reporter
   b. a research student
   c. an inquisitive tourist

2. What does the speaker ask for as the price for her story?
   a. Nothing. She has been longing for the chance to tell her story.
   b. The price is the listener's soul.
   c. A couple of drinks at least.

3. This story has a very clear turning point. At which sentence does it occur?
   a. *'I was born in 1950, yes it seems a lifetime ago.'*
   b. *'I would find myself rising into the sky above the great oaks.'*
   c. *'The shadow would come, the sun would die…'*

4. The fairies wore dresses of red poppies. Why are red poppies special?
   a. They have a very short life.
   b. They are a flower traditionally worn by fairies.
   c. They are often used as a symbol of remembrance at war memorials.

5. Which is the overriding sentiment in this story?
   a. a sense of loss
   b. a feeling of universal guilt
   c. a belief in supernatural beings

Crossword puzzle

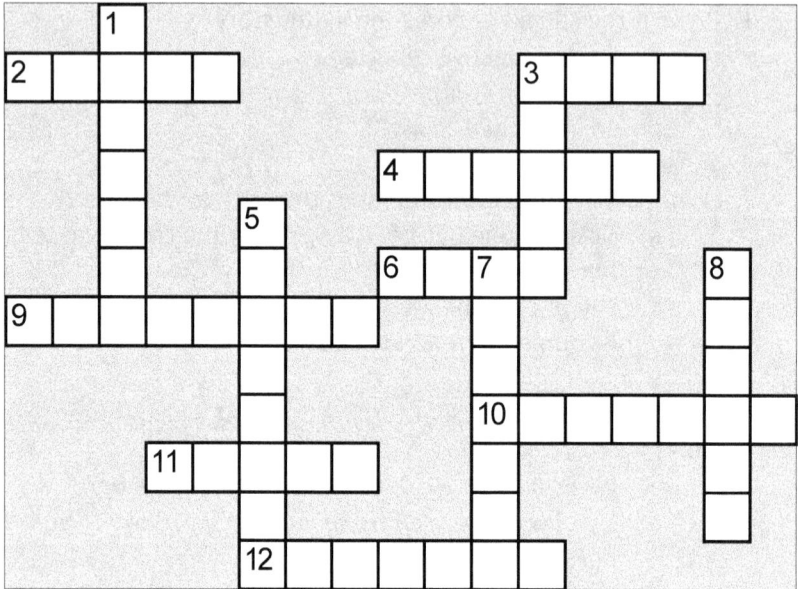

ACROSS

2 turn around and around
3 turn around a point
4 circular decoration
6 vegetable-based fuel
9 monument
10 tall pillar of stone
11 repeat over and over
12 long, flowing hair

DOWN

1 traveller to a holy place
3 wooden stick
5 not serious enough
7 move around a central axis
8 written research report

Picture quiz – fairy tale creatures

A Unscramble the words below and match them to the pictures.

1   2   3

4   5   6

APRELUNCH   DIMERAM   FLE   YAFIR   BLINGO   NEIGE

Write the words below.

1 _____   2 _____   3 _____

4 _____   5 _____   6 _____

B Which of the above is associated with...

1 Aladdin (   ) **2** Ireland (   ) **3** (   ) the sea
4 the forest (   ) **5** Peter Pan (   ) **6** wickedness (   )

That's Cricket!

by Dorothy Elchlepp

— ☙ ❧ —

The sun seems to shine a bit brighter somehow when it beams on a village cricket match. The broad green glistens like emerald against the shade of encircling trees, and the cricketers move through their ritual clad in dazzling white.

All this came back to me one nostalgic September, no, not in England but in a small town in southern Germany, only a few miles from Freiburg. Denzlingen had been twinned with North Hykeham in Lincolnshire for ten years. A team consisting of young expat Englishmen, Australians, Irishmen, Scots and two Sri Lankans had formed a cricket club and offered to play a match against a team consisting of players only from Sri Lanka.

The German spectators, eager to know more about our national game, were to be given a commentary over a loud speaker. One couldn't expect a pitch in the middle of a football field to live up to any of our village greens, and a piece of matting had been laid down between the wickets. I soon realised that the public were getting impatient.

As a girl, I had watched the game so often. My brother played for Sussex in the fifties and I had often accompanied my father to Lords or the Oval for a Test Match. Two nephews played for Eastbourne College. In other words, I knew the rules.

Back to Denzlingen. All eyes were riveted on the centre of the green where a young man abruptly leapt forward in giant strides, swung a stiff arm and hurled a small red ball at blistering speed towards a target formed by three upright sticks (the stumps) joined at the top by two bails.

My immediate neighbours in the recreation ground stand started to put questions to me, so I explained that the man guarding the wicket was the batsman who meets the missile with his bat and a thwack sends the ball towards one of the crouching fielders. He snaps it up barehanded and the batsman decides it's not safe to run. This is cricket; he doesn't have to.

My neighbours started to show interest. I continued and gradually the picture emerged. Two wickets set 22 yards apart, each defended by a batsman, two bowlers attacking the wickets, one bowls an over of six balls, then fields while his mate bowls from the other end of the pitch. This bowler tries with either a fast or a slow spinning delivery to bounce the ball past the batsman and demolish the wicket. If a batsman tries to block or swipe the ball and it strikes him instead of his bat, the umpire rules 'leg before wicket' and he's OUT! If he knocks a ball over the boundary he gets a six. If a flying ball is caught, the batsman is OUT. When ten of a team's eleven men are out, the 'innings' ends and the other side comes in to bat.

Well, I thought, that's enough for a start and I felt I had stirred up some interest. However, I feel that cricket will never catch on in Germany; they simply get too impatient with slow play.

Cricket, traditionally England's national game, has a longer history than most team games and its basic rules have scarcely altered since the 1700's and the game was old then. Royal household accounts show that Prince Edward, later Edward II, played it at Westminster in 1300.

Cricket has provided one expression that is now heard in many connections, that is 'hat trick', which dates back to the days when cricketers wore top hats. Any player who took three wickets with three successive balls was presented with a white top hat.

The old game still stirs English hearts. Newspaper headlines proclaim the loss of a Test Match with words that frighten foreign investors: "ENGLAND TOPPLES", one recently screamed in large capitals.

On that day in Denzlingen, as a thwack of willow was met by a mild ripple of applause, I couldn't help thinking that here, on the edge of the Black Forest, was a little piece of England.

— ❧ ☙ —

Words and phrases

glistens like emerald	shines like a green jewel
shade	shadow
clad	wearing
nostalgic	thinking affectionately of the past
spectators	people watching the event
eager	interested, keen
pitch	central strip of the cricket field between the wickets
live up to	be equal to or as good as
wickets	set of sticks that is bowled at
impatient	annoyed at waiting
riveted on	fixed on
strides	steps
hurled	threw hard
blistering speed	very fast
target	something that is aimed at
recreation ground	open public space for games etc.
thwack	sound made when two solid objects hit each other hard
demolish	knock down
boundary	perimeter of the cricket field
topples	becomes unstable

Food for thought

1. Cricket is the name of the game described here, but the word is also used as a synonym for...
   a. patience
   b. fair play
   c. anything with complicated rules

2. What impression does the writer have of the Germans in the story?
   a. They can be rather impatient.
   b. They are very interested in all kinds of sport.
   c. The find cricket fascinating.

3. The rules of cricket...
   a. were laid down by Edward II.
   b. have become more complicated in recent years
   c. have not changed very much over the years

4. Nowadays, the term 'hat trick' ...
   a. is regarded as old-fashioned.
   b. can be heard in many contexts.
   c. is used mainly in cricket.

5. Which adjective best describes this story?
   a. sentimental
   b. humorous
   c. cynical

Word search

Find the words in the grid. Words can go horizontally, vertically or diagonally in any direction. When you are done, the unused letters in the grid will spell out a <u>hidden message</u>, reading from left to right, top to bottom. There will be a few letters left over.

```
      A  C  R  I  C  B  O  U  N  D  A  R  Y
   T  G  K  E  T  G  R  O  E  M  E  R  A  L  D
   E  N  U     N  O  I  T  A  E  R  C  E  R  N  D
   K  I  I  N  S  A  F  S  C  L  A  D     L     A
   C  R  T  P  O     H  C  T  I  P  I  E  C  N  E
   I  E  S  O  F  S  E  A  R  R  T  H     W  E  I
   W  T  P  T  H  S  T  O  M     I  T  E     T  B
   U  S  E  I  L  D  I  A  E  N  N  D  H  G  S  S
   A  I  C  R  O  U  N  D  L  E  D  S  E  T  I  I
   T  L  T  M  T     A     I  G  I  T  A     L  N
   N  B  A  L  P  H  K  T  D  L  I  R  K  E  G  J
   F  D  T  M  S  B  A  C  O  N  G  C  A  L  H  W
   J  D  O  G  B  P  K  M  A  E  U  G     J  U  P
   M  K  R  R  M  N  E  V  T  W  E  O  P  K  R  J
   B  W     I  R  D  T     T  R  H  V  R  K  L  F
   L  N  T  O  P  P  L  E        T  K  G     K
```

blistering	emerald	nostalgic	stride
boundary	glisten	pitch	target
clad	ground	recreation	thwack
demolish	hurl	shade	topple
eager	impatient	spectator	wicket

Hidden message: ....

Picture quiz – sports

A Match the names of the sports to the pictures.

1    2    3    4

5    6    7    8

| CANOEING | BADMINTON | BOWLING | JUDO |
| BASEBALL | ARCHERY | GOLF | ICE HOCKEY |

1 _____ 2 _____ 3 _____ 4 _____

5 _____ 6 _____ 7 _____ 8 _____

B Match the words below with the sports above.
1 bat ( )   **2** puck ( )   **3** shuttlecock ( )   **4** dojo ( )
5 paddle ( )   **6** alley ( )   **7** bow ( )   **8** hole ( )

Flitzo

by Anthony Curtis

— ❧ ❧ —

Jenny handed the letter to her husband.

"Here, Jim, read the last paragraph," she said, knowing how much he hated letters from Aunt Emma.

"… and now for the exciting part.

I know you'll never believe me (nobody ever does), but there seems to be a plague of bluebottles in our house. With the weather we're having at the moment, they must be reproducing like rabbits. We've sprayed them with that special spray which is not supposed to upset the balance of nature. You know, Jenny. Flitzo. It's supposed to be the best thing there is. It gets rid of flies, mosquitos, bugs and cockroaches, with no risk of poisoning ourselves. But no matter how often we spray, for every fly we get rid of, it seems that two take its place.

And that's not all. I'm certain that the creatures are learning to hide. Fred goes along with this. He's always remarked on how dumb bluebottles are, but he's not so certain now. They normally just sit there and let themselves be pulverised … "

He read on …

"… they seem to hide in every nook and cranny. We've installed mosquito nets on all our windows, but they still keep on coming. I shudder to think how many maggots are crawling about in the wainscoting. We went to the Sanitary Department last week, but they were on strike, and still are. Fred says the flies have probably built up a resistance to Flitzo. I do hope not. It's terribly expensive."

There followed the usual greetings to the family and "... why don't you visit us anymore? Love, Aunt Emma."

Jim handed the letter back to his wife.

"Overdoing it a bit, isn't she?"

"I suppose you're right," said Jenny. "I can't really accept her suggestion that flies are getting clever enough to conceal themselves."

Jim pondered for a while and then said, "Yes, it does sound improbable, doesn't it? But if it were true, and I'm not saying for one moment that it is, it wouldn't be very good for us, would it?"

Jim laughed nervously.

"What are you talking about, Jim?"

"I once heard a professor on the radio say that if insects ever achieve intelligence, our intelligence that is, the human race will probably vanish within a week.

And the irony of it all is, the world itself would be saved from further pollution. He also said something about there being no final stage of evolution. That all our meddling with genetic engineering and cloning will eventually change the natural order of things. There'll be new evolutionary stages, and heaven knows what will happen then."

Jenny shuddered. "You're making me nervous, Jim. And all because of a stupid letter."

Jim laughed. "I was only kidding, darling. Let's forget it. Aunt Emma's obviously trying to draw attention to herself."

They promptly forgot the matter and played cards for the rest of the evening.

Having given the television the night off, they failed to learn that thousands of wasps had been terrorising people in the southern counties.

That night, although Jim slept soundly, Jenny, more influenced by Aunt Emma's letter than she would have liked to admit, kept her eyes open for bluebottles. But, of course, there weren't any, and eventually, she, too, drifted off to sleep.

She was awakened in the wee small hours by a buzzing sound. She switched on the light and surveyed the walls and the ceiling. Nothing. She was about to switch off the light when it occurred to her that she had not looked behind the bed, which was not completely against the wall. She did so. Six extremely large mosquitos clung to the wall as if they were waiting for something.

Shocked, Jenny softly opened and closed the bedroom door, and went down to the kitchen.

The Flitzo was in the cupboard under the sink, which seemed to be infested with woodlice.

Back in the bedroom, she sprayed the mosquitos. They fell onto the carpet. Placing the spray can on the dressing table, Jenny got into bed again.

An hour later, she was awakened by a buzzing sound. She turned the light on and surveyed the walls and the ceiling. No mosquitos. She looked behind the bed. Nothing on the wall or on the carpet. She began to scratch her neck. It was itching terribly and in more places than one. Jim slept soundlessly on.

In panic, she searched and searched. No mosquitos. Anywhere.

By now, her neck was considerably swollen and Jenny was beginning to feel drowsy. She lay on the bed. Very soon she slipped into a coma …

From a small air grille behind the dressing table, a dozen mosquitos appeared and zoomed towards the bed.

"Here is enough blood for a million offspring," thought one.

"Thanks to Flitzo," thought another.

And without opening their long mouths, the rest of the mosquitos agreed.

— ❧ ❧ —

Words and phrases

plague	large number, invasion, infestation
bluebottle	large fly with dark blue body
balance of nature	ecological stability
gets rid of	kills, destroys
bugs	small animals, including insects
poisoning ourselves	harming our bodies
pulverised	crushed, killed, flattened
nook and cranny	cavity, crack, corner
maggots	small worm-like creatures that turn into flies
wainscoting	wooden panelling on walls
conceal themselves	hide, stay out of sight
pondered	thought about, considered
vanish	disappear, die out
pollution	poisonous or dirty substances that damage the environment
meddling	messing, interfering
surveyed	inspected
infested with	crawling with, full of
drowsy	sleepy
air grille	ventilation grid
offspring	children, (here) baby mosquitos

Food for thought

1. Which problem does Aunt Emma describe in her letter?
   a. There are flies everywhere and they seem to have become more intelligent.
   b. She has wasted a lot of money on Flitzo, which simply does not work.
   c. Her husband did not believe her when she told him about the flies.

2. Which opinion did the professor on the radio express?
   a. Insects are cleverer than humans.
   b. If insects become cleverer than humans, humans will quickly die out.
   c. Insects will never become cleverer than humans.

3. When Jenny went to bed...
   a. she knew that wasps had been terrorising people in the southern counties.
   b. she had forgotten all about the insect problem.
   c. she stayed awake for a while, watching out for bluebottles.

4. Why did Jenny go downstairs?
   a. To get the Flitzo.
   b. To check for more insects.
   c. To find out what was in the cupboard under the sink.

5. At the end of the story, it seems that
   a. only the mosquitos have become more intelligent.
   b. Aunt Emma was right to be concerned.
   c. Jenny has been having a nightmare.

Crossword puzzle

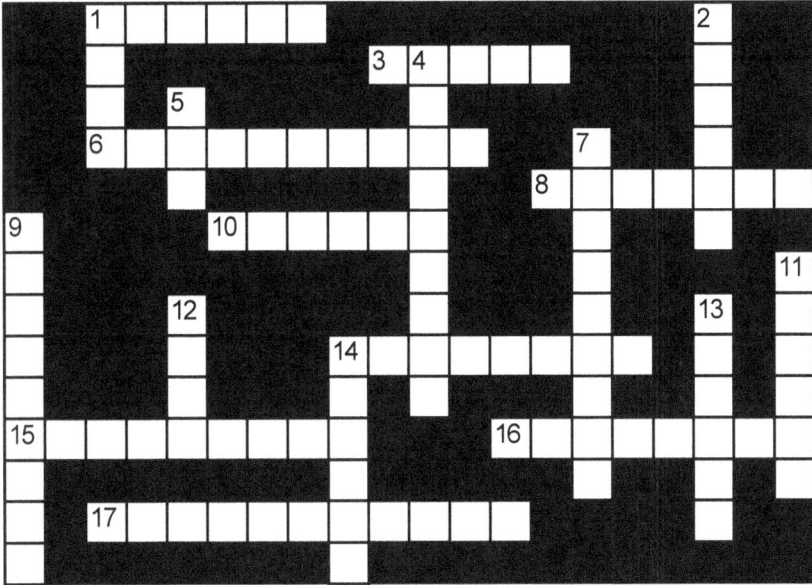

ACROSS

1 sleepy
3 liquid applied as a jet
6 large fly
8 hide
10 infestation
14 blood-sucking insect
15 children
16 small crawling creatures with a flat, elliptical body
17 wooden panelling

DOWN

1 stupid
2 consider
4 crush, kill
5 small animal
7 environmental poison
9 big brown flat insect pest
11 inspect
12 stinging insect
13 disappear
14 small worm-like creature

Picture quiz – insects

A Match the names of insects to the pictures.

BUMBLEBEE   DRAGONFLY   BLUEBOTTLE   FLEA
BEETLE   MOSQUITO   MOTH   GRASSHOPPER

1 _____ 2 _____ 3 _____ 4 _____

5 _____ 6 _____ 7 _____ 8 _____

B Which of the above...

1 chirps ( )   **2** collects pollen ( )   **3** likes blood ( )
4 creeps ( )   **5** is a kind of housefly ( ) **6** is very small
and can jump a long way ( )   **7** eats clothes ( ) **8** has
a mythical beast in its name ( )

Answer key

The Farmer's Son

Food for thought
1 a   **2** c   **3** b   **4** c   **5** b

Crossword puzzle

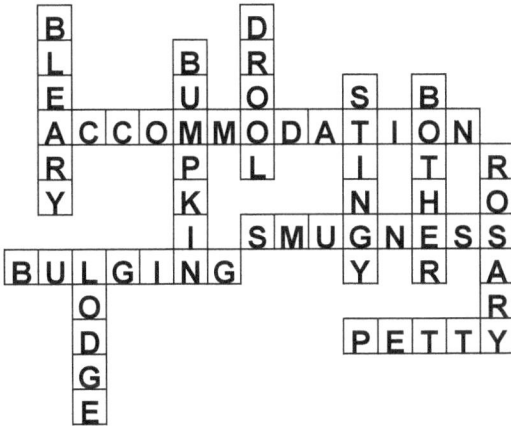

```
B       D
L     B R
E     U O     S B
A C C O M M O D A T I O N
R     P L     I T     R
Y     K       N H     O
      I   S M U G N E S S
B U L G I N G     Y R     A
  O                       R
  D           P E T T Y
  G
  E
```

Picture quiz
A
1 DONKEY   **2** TURKEY   **3** PIG   **4** ROOSTER   **5** COW   **6** DUCK

B
1 (3)   **2** (1)   **3** (6)   **4** (5)   **5** (4)   **6** (2)

The Scarlet Dress

Food for thought
1 b **2** c **3** a **4** b **5** a
Word search

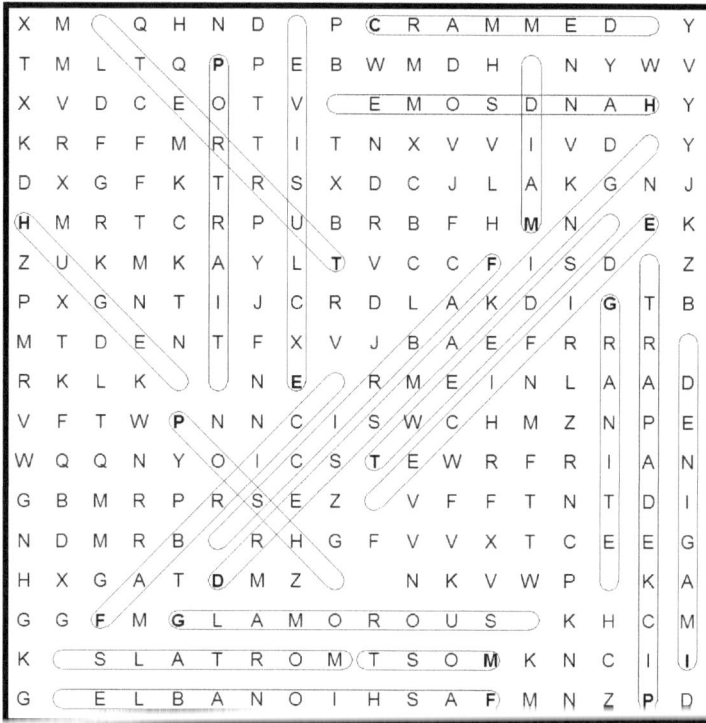

Picture quiz

A

1 SKIRT **2** BLOUSE **3** BRA **4** DRESS **5** CORSET **6** TOP

B

1 (4) **2** (1) **3** (2) **4** (6) **5** (5) **6** (3)

Ghostly Laughter

Food for thought
1 b   **2** c   **3** b   **4** c   **5** a

Crossword puzzle

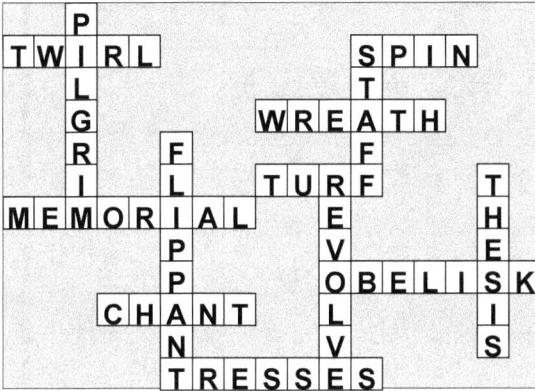

```
     P
T W I R L           S P I N
     L              T
     G       W R E A T H
     R   F          F
     I   L   T U R F         T
M E M O R I A L     E         H
         P          V         E
         P          O B E L I S K
     C H A N T      L         I
         N          V         S
         T R E S S E S
```

Picture quiz

A

1 FAIRY **2** GOBLIN **3** GENIE

4 MERMAID **5** LEPRECHAUN **6** ELF

B

1 (3) **2** (5) **3** (4) **4** (6) **5** (1) **6** (2)

67

That's Cricket!

Food for thought
1 b   **2** a   **3** c   **4** b   **5** a

Word search

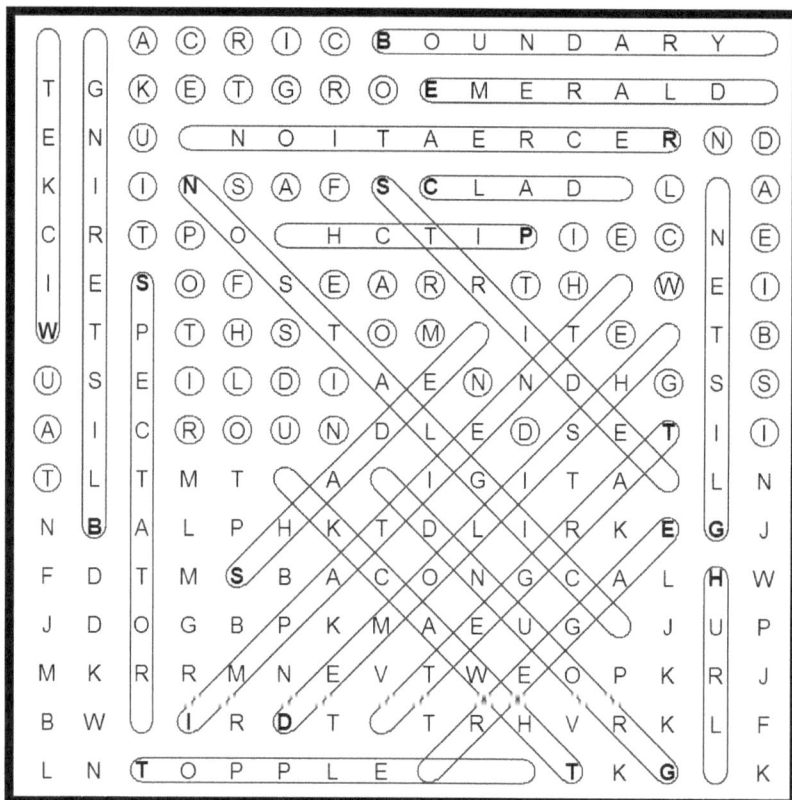

Hidden message: 'A cricket ground is a flat piece of earth with some buildings around it.' - Richie Benaud (1930 - 2015), Australian cricketer and captain of Australia 1958-1964

Picture quiz

A

1 ICE HOCKEY   **2** GOLF   **3** BADMINTON   4 BOWLING
5 ARCHERY   **6** CANOEING   **7** JUDO   **8** BASEBALL

B

1 (8)   **2** (1)   **3** (3)   **4** (7)   **5** (6)   **6** (4)   **7** (5)   **8** (2)

Flitzo

Food for thought

1 a   **2** b   **3** c   **4** a   **5** b

Crossword puzzle

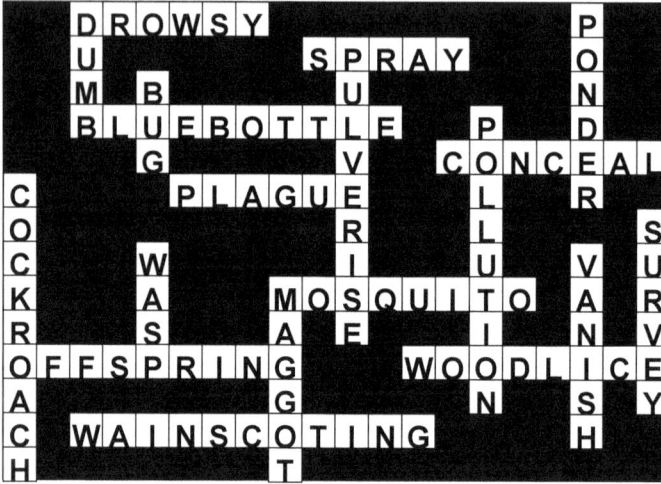

Picture quiz

A

1 BEETLE   **2** MOTH   **3** DRAGONFLY   **4** FLEA   **5** MOSQUITO
6 BUMBLEBEE   **7** GRASSHOPPER   **8** BLUEBOTTLE

B

1 (7)   **2** (6)   **3** (5)   **4** (1)   **5** (8)   **6** (4)   **7** (2)   **8** (3)

Further titles from LinguaBooks

IN A STRANGE LAND

Short Stories for Creative Learning
Andrzej Cirocki and Alicia Peña Calvo   ISBN 978-3734789465

IN A STRANGE LAND is a collection of four original short stories which provide teachers with motivating and engaging classroom material at the CEFR B2 to C1 level and young adult learners with thought-provoking narratives and characters to whom they can relate.

This gripping teenage fiction encourages readers to use their imagination and interact with the texts in a variety of educational and experimental ways.

The stories are supported by creative tasks which enable students to integrate their various language skills, exploit computer technology, practise learning strategies and exercise autonomy.

Audio recordings of the stories are available on two separate CDs which are suitable for classroom use and can also be listened to for pleasure.

Academic Presenting and Presentations

A preparation course for university students
Peter Levrai and Averil Bolster   ISBN 978-3734783678

This practical training course is designed to help students cultivate academic presentation skills and deal with the variety of presentation tasks they may need to master during their studies.

The material is suitable for a global audience and can be used in a wide range of academic contexts since the content not only helps learners develop their presentation skills in English but also considers wider topics relevant to English for Academic Purposes, such as principles of research and the risk of plagiarism.

The accompanying online video presentations enable learners to immerse themselves still further in the material presented and witness first-hand the impact of the techniques illustrated.

A separate Teacher's Book is also available: ISBN: 978-3741242090

Developing Learner Autonomy Through Tasks
Research, Theory, Practice

Andrzej Cirocki   ISBN 978-1-911369-01-1

At the heart of this study is the fostering of learner autonomy in the language classroom, in particular how learner autonomy can be developed through pedagogical tasks. The work focuses on four different approaches: learner-related, classroom-related, resource-related and technology-related.

Developing Learner Autonomy through Tasks combines classroom theory, research and practice, all of which are immersed in the philosophy of social constructivism, whereby knowledge and learning are seen as both the context for and the result of human interaction.

"This is the book everyone in the field has been waiting for. It is the product of excellent classroom research... highly engaging, relevant, readable, and above all, practical in its handling of the issues."
- Prof. John McRae, University of Nottingham, UK

Controversies in ELT
What you always wanted to know about teaching English
but were afraid to ask
Maurice Claypole   ISBN 978-1-911369-00-4

This thought-provoking and informative collection of essays covers a broad spectrum of topics relating to English language teaching, including chapters on The Death Of the Communicative Approach, Teaching the Language of Sex and Teaching English in Second Life.

Also released for the first time in book form are chapters on the author's unique insight into the correlation between language, set theory and fractal mathematics - and the consequences for English teachers.

"This book provides a refreshing look at old concepts, opens our eyes to new perspectives and encourages teachers to venture along new paths."
- Elke Schulth, ELTAS, Germany

"Interesting... instructive and - not least - fun to read. A brilliant book!"
- Nick Michelioudakis, TESOL Greece

www.ingramcontent.com/pod-product-compliance
Lightning Source LLC
LaVergne TN
LVHW051709080426
835511LV00017B/2818